WARN/NG:
W/LD WEATHER AHEAD

by **Theo Baker**

Grosset & Dunlap
An Imprint of Penguin Random House

To James Lovelock, creator of the Gaia Hypothesis, and as always, my girls:
Sarah, Anarres, and Elettra—TB

GROSSET & DUNLAP
Penguin Young Readers Group
An Imprint of Penguin Random House LLC

Photo credits: front cover: © sytilin/Thinkstock; page 1: © Image Source Pink/Thinkstock; page 2: © Serg_Velusceac/Thinkstock; page 3: © USAP, Photograph by Emily Walker, Courtesy of the National Science Foundation, U.S. Antarctic Program; page 4: © Gwenvidig/ Thinkstock; pages 6–7: © UCARI/Thinkstock; pages 8–9: © Nastco/Thinkstock; pages 10–11: © Mr_Twister/Thinkstock; pages 12–13: © Paolo74s/Thinkstock; pages 14–15: © Comstock/ Thinkstock; pages 16–17: © PicturetakerJoseph/Thinkstock; pages 18–19: © Samuel D. Barricklow/Getty; pages 20–21: © Coprid/Thinkstock; pages 22–23: © Stocktrek Images/ Getty; pages 24–25: Courtesy of NOAA; pages 26–27: © Brendan Delany/Thinkstock; pages 28–29, 30–31: Courtesy of NASA; page 32: © Matteo Colombo/Getty

Text copyright © 2017 by Theo Baker. All rights reserved. Published by Grosset & Dunlap, an imprint of Penguin Random House LLC, 345 Hudson Street, New York, New York 10014. GROSSET & DUNLAP is a trademark of Penguin Random House LLC.
Manufactured in China.

Library of Congress Cataloging-in-Publication Data is available.

ISBN 9780448488738   10 9 8 7 6 5 4 3 2

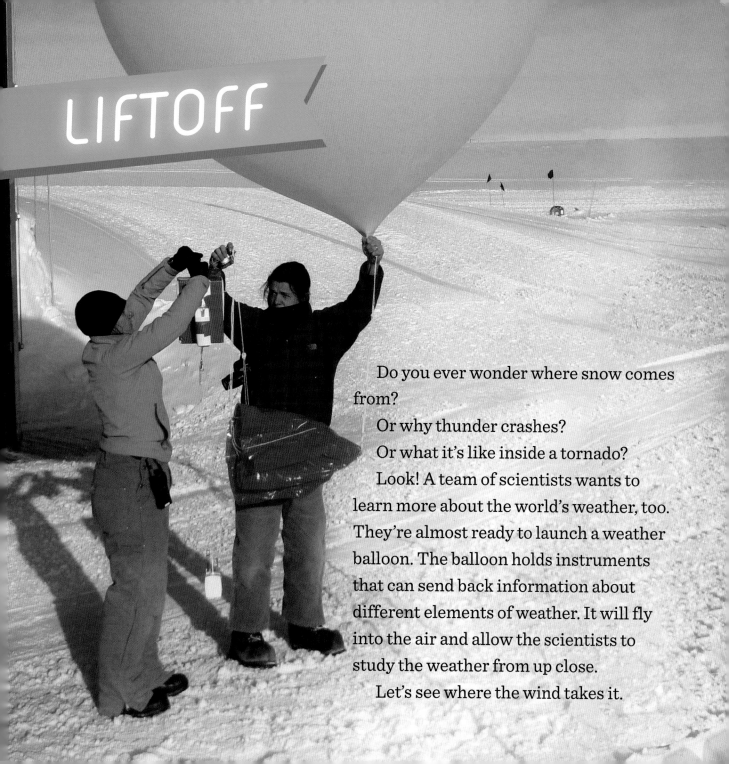

LIFTOFF

Do you ever wonder where snow comes from?

Or why thunder crashes?

Or what it's like inside a tornado?

Look! A team of scientists wants to learn more about the world's weather, too. They're almost ready to launch a weather balloon. The balloon holds instruments that can send back information about different elements of weather. It will fly into the air and allow the scientists to study the weather from up close.

Let's see where the wind takes it.

WIND

The weather balloon climbs swiftly into the sky. As it rises, it begins to drift across the landscape with a warm wind from the west.

Wind is moving air. The wind can move gently, such as a cool afternoon breeze. Or it can blow with the violence of a hurricane. But no matter how it moves, wind is the driving force behind all of the world's weather.

Wind happens whenever warm air and cool air mix together. Warm air and cool air are as opposite as night and day. Warm air is light and energetic. Cool air is heavy and sluggish. And when the two meet, they push and pull and spin one another in strange and complex ways.

Our planet's spin also causes wind. At the equator—the middle of the planet—Earth spins around and around at over one thousand miles per hour. Though we don't feel the movement, this tremendous speed whips up the winds and sends them streaming around the world.

WEATHER WONDER

Earth is surrounded by the *atmosphere*, a protective envelope of gas. The world's weather happens in the *troposphere*—the lowest layer of Earth's atmosphere.

CLOUDS

The weather balloon climbs high into the cool, thin air. The weather balloon isn't the only thing rising with the wind. The wind is also carrying dust, pollen, bacteria, and even baby spiders. Most importantly, the wind is carrying microscopic droplets of water called *water vapor*. When there's enough water vapor in the air, and the temperature is just right, something amazing happens.

All around the weather balloon, water droplets begin attaching themselves to all those pieces of dust and bacteria. Then suddenly, as if by magic, clouds appear.

There are three main types of clouds. Cumulus clouds are the most common. They are white fluffy clouds that look like cotton candy. Stratus clouds are long, flat gray clouds that blanket the sky on gloomy days. And cirrus clouds are curly wisps of ice crystals high in the sky.

WEATHER WONDER

The water droplets that form clouds are so small and light that you could drink fifty billion of them in one big sip!

SNOW

The weather balloon is sucked into a big cloud bulging over the mountains. Cumulus clouds may look like harmless fluff balls from the ground, but inside, they are chaotic. Columns of wind race up and down, and side to side, and the weather balloon is pulled up higher and higher by the wind.

The temperature drops below freezing.

And then, for reasons scientists don't fully understand yet, a tiny droplet of water freezes into a six-sided ice crystal. In the blink of an eye, this single crystal draws other droplets to it, which freeze together. When this growing ice crystal is heavy enough, it falls through the cloud, triggering other cloud droplets to freeze together.

The cloud is now full of snow. Many snowflakes get pulled up high into the sky, where they become cirrus clouds. The rest fall through the quiet air as snowflakes.

WEATHER WONDER

Snowflakes are made of air and ice, but mostly air. The amount of moisture in the air helps determine the shape of each snowflake. When there is moisture in the air, more intricate snowflake patterns form, while drier air produces snowflakes with simpler shapes.

RAIN

The weather balloon drifts to the other side of the mountain, where it's warmer. Now the cloud is made up of both water droplets and snowflakes. The snowflakes are at the top of the cloud, almost 15,000 feet high. They continue falling through the cloud, but whenever they meet warmer air, they melt into raindrops. The raindrops grow bigger and bigger by sticking to other cloud droplets as they fall.

Raindrops don't actually look like teardrops. They look like regular balls at first. But as they get heavier, they flatten out into a pancake shape. Once the raindrops leave the clouds, they fall to the earth at 7 to 18 miles per hour.

WEATHER WONDER

All the rain that falls to the ground eventually turns to water vapor and gets lifted back to the sky. And if you took all the water vapor in the sky and spread it evenly around the world, it would make a puddle about an inch deep.

THUNDERSTORM

The rain cloud breaks apart. A hot wind has begun to blow. The land below is also hot, and the air is moist. The sky has a strange yellow-and-gray color to it, and everything feels electric. The weather balloon is surrounded by an eerie blue glow. Just ahead, a cumulonimbus—the king of the clouds—is stretching toward the top of the sky. It is a thick, dark, towering monster, and the weather balloon is heading right for it!

The wind picks up, and with a violent gust of hot air, the balloon is sucked up into the center of the thundercloud.

The sky goes black. The winds scream. Huge raindrops soak the balloon in seconds as it is tossed and turned and shot up at the cloud with frightening speed. Ice freezes around the balloon in an instant. The very top of the cloud is over 35,000 feet high. And above the cloud, violent winds swoosh downward, flattening the cloud top into an anvil shape. The cloud flickers with electric blue-and-white light.

Suddenly, a massive lightning stroke explodes and thunder cracks.

THUNDER AND LIGHTNING

Lightning has filled people with fear and wonder since the beginning of time. But even today, there is still much we do not know about this strange light in the sky.

For reasons that aren't completely understood yet, thunderclouds become electrically charged. And so does the ground beneath the storm. When the thundercloud is ready to burst with electricity, a weak and invisible lightning stroke zigzags out of the storm, down to the ground. Once it touches the ground, a powerful flash of energy races back up into the cloud. This "return stroke" is the one we see. It's not simply one stroke, either: A single flash is actually many different flashes. Lightning bolts heat the air around them to as much as 50,000 degrees Fahrenheit, five times as hot as the surface of the sun.

Science knows somewhat more about thunder than lightning. A lightning bolt's amazing heat causes the air around the stroke to rapidly expand and contract. The air is moving faster than the speed of sound, and when two masses of air meet, they pound each other, like a drumstick smashing a drum. Sometimes the "drumming" is low and rumbling, and sometimes it sounds like an explosion.

WEATHER WONDER

Sometimes, lightning strokes melt the ground and form a hollow tube called a fulgurite. They are so beautiful that many wear fulgurites as jewelry.

HAIL

Conditions within the thundercloud have become more extreme. The weather balloon is flung up, shot down, and spun around wildly in heavy turbulence. The lightning flashes now seem almost green, and so does the entire cloud. The balloon is battered with what sounds like small rocks. The rain has turned to hail!

Hailstones are not delicate like snowflakes. Instead, they are ragged and tough. They only come from the roughest thunderclouds.

They form when falling rain is flung back to the freezing top of the cloud by powerful updrafts of wind. At the top, the rain freezes into an ice ball. Then the storm bounces the ice ball around the thundercloud like a pinball. Everywhere it goes, it picks up new ice layers, and it grows bigger and heavier until the storm can no longer support its weight.

Most hailstones are pea-size, and fall to the ground at about twenty miles per hour. But hail can be much bigger. And the bigger the hail, the faster it falls. Hailstones the size of oranges can plummet to the ground at over 100 miles per hour, and they do horrendous damage.

WEATHER WONDER

Sometimes giant chunks of ice fall in clear skies. These *clear sky ice fall events* are a complete mystery. Occasionally they can drop ice chunks weighing over 100 pounds.

TORNADO

The storm is not finished yet. It has become a *supercell*, a rotating storm system with strong updrafts. A hissing, whooshing roar rises up from beneath the weather balloon, along with a strange smell. Down below, a spinning vortex opens in the cloud layer. A funnel cloud drops down, its walls swirling with lightning. The weather balloon is directly over a tornado!

Science does not understand why tornadoes form, nor can science predict where they'll strike, how long they'll last, or how big and destructive they will be.
Most tornadoes are about 75 feet across and have winds of about 100 miles per hour. But some monster storms can spawn a tornado over a mile wide, with winds of over 300 miles per hour.

Tornadoes can lift cars, pull the bark off trees, and destroy whole towns. Many scientists suspect that a tornado's destructive power doesn't come from its fierce winds, but from its low pressure. There is so little air within a tornado that it is like a vacuum cleaner, sucking everything up.

RAINBOWS

The tornado has broken up, and so has
the supercell storm, leaving behind only a light
drizzle. Sunbeams peek through the clouds, and a
rainbow arcs across the sky. The lower the sun is in the
sky, the higher the rainbow seems from the ground.
Seeing a rainbow from the air is truly a thing of beauty.
If the sun is just about to set, and you are high enough, the
rainbow isn't an arch at all, but a complete circle!

You can't touch a rainbow, nor can you find the end of it. The closer
you try to get to one, the farther it moves away. A rainbow isn't actually
there. A rainbow is, rather, a fantastic trick of light.

We see rainbows when sunlight
passes through rain at an angle. Each
little raindrop changes the light's direction
and scatters it. Although sunlight seems "white,"
it is really a mixture of all the colors in a rainbow: red,
orange, yellow, green, blue, indigo, and violet. A rainbow is
unmixed sunlight.

Our weather balloon has been through a lot. It floats gently
down to the waiting scientists on the ground. But the scientists
aren't done learning about the weather yet. They look up and see a
weather plane flying overhead, above the rainbow.

HURRICANE

This weather plane is loaded with instruments. Now it is flying toward the ocean. But the ocean has a strange, flat look. Long, rolling waves pound the shore only four to five times a minute, instead of the usual seven to eight times. On the horizon a looming mountain of black clouds covers half the sky. A hurricane is coming.

This expert pilot is going to fly the weather plane right into it.

A hurricane is a ferocious storm that unleashes heavy thunderstorms, searing winds, and devastating floods. The hurricane's power is fueled by the eye of the storm. The eye is usually ten to twenty miles wide. Within it, the air is heavy and hot, much hotter than the surrounding storm. The air pressure is also very low, and this sucks up seawater to the eye. The spiraling winds inside the eye whip up this water and send immense, rolling swells in every direction. And if the eye of the storm reaches the shore, a wall of water floods the coast.

Once a hurricane hits land, it will lose most of its strength within a day or two. Without warm water to feed it, the hurricane loses steam, and quickly fades back into the air.

WEATHER WONDER

Scientists grade hurricanes on a scale of 1 to 5, with 5 being the most powerful. Any hurricane above a category 3 is incredibly destructive. Category 5 storms have sustained winds of over 154 miles per hour.

JET STREAMS AND OCEAN WEATHER

The weather plane flies through the hurricane several times, gathering data. Then the plane starts climbing, heading up and up until it reaches the polar jet stream. This is a long, thin tube of wind that travels around the world, with winds between 100 and 200 miles per hour. These winds will give the weather plane a boost of speed as its instruments collect information about the oceans below.

Most of Earth's surface is water. This is a good thing, because water is a remarkable substance. Unlike land or air, water heats and cools very slowly. The ocean's steady and mild temperature keeps the planet's winds from getting too hot or too cold. And since the wind goes everywhere, the planet's overall temperature is kept stable and mild. Without the ocean, Earth would broil in the sunlight, and freeze at night.

COLD PLACES

The polar jet stream guides the weather plane over the frozen island of Greenland. Greenland is above the Arctic Circle, and within a few hundred miles of the North Pole. Almost the entire island is covered with a sheet of ice nearly two miles thick.

Ice and snow cover roughly 10 percent of the planet's surface, and play a crucial role in the planet's climate, especially the ice caps at the South and North Poles. Ice and snow act like heat mirrors: They bounce most of the sun's heat back into space. Winds kicking off the ice cool the planet.

Another cool thing about ice is that it floats. This means that no matter how cold the air is, beneath the ice the water never drops much below 32 degrees Fahrenheit. This provides a chilly but livable climate for life under the ice.

WEATHER WONDER

Only 3 percent of the planet's water is fresh, drinkable water. But most of the freshwater is locked up in glaciers and ice sheets.

DESERTS

While the weather plane gathers data about the North Pole, astronauts aboard the International Space Station are watching a dust storm sweep across the Sahara Desert, the world's largest desert. One of the station's instruments is collecting data about the dust, so scientists can better understand how dust and other particles in the air affect the climate.

A desert is a place with so little rain or snow that few animals and plants can live there. Most of the world's deserts line the middle of the planet, along the equator. But deserts can be cold, too. In fact, Antarctica, the island continent home to the South Pole, is a desert. Though it is covered with ice, it is too frigid there for water vapor to escape from the ice and form rain or snow clouds.

About a third of Earth's land is covered in desert, and the deserts are spreading.

WEATHER WONDER

The hottest land temperature ever recorded was just under 135 degrees Fahrenheit in Furnace Creek, California. The coldest was recorded by NASA in eastern Antarctica, where it got down to negative 135.8 degrees Fahrenheit.

GLOBAL
WARMING

The International Space Station orbits Earth once every ninety minutes. During those ninety minutes, the astronauts pass over deserts, glaciers, oceans, snow, clouds, water—all the weather the world has to offer. From space, it is easy for the astronauts to see that every weather event flows into the next one. Everything is connected. All of the world's weather is part of one global pattern.

We are currently living through a new type of weather pattern: global warming. Human industry—cars, factories, power plants—creates a lot of waste like carbon dioxide and methane gas, and pumps these *greenhouse gases* into the atmosphere. Once these gases get to the atmosphere, they act like a thick blanket, trapping heat and warming the planet.

No one knows exactly how global warming will affect the future's weather, but it could change the world as we know it: Ice caps could melt and cause the oceans to flood coastal cities, the oceans could become too hot and acidic to support complex life, and the spreading deserts could swallow up all our farmlands.

The good news is that people have the power to stop and then reverse global warming. It will be difficult, but not impossible. The choice is ours.

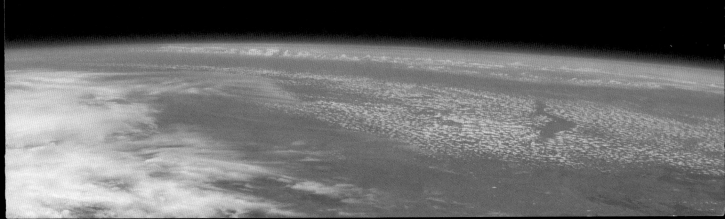

Earth is home to all sorts of wild and wonderful weather. Some of it is pleasant and calm, while some of it is violent and frightening. One thing to remember, though, is that all of it is connected.